THE ART OF *Shaping* *Shrubs* *Trees* AND *Other Plants*

THE ART OF *Shaping*

Shrubs Trees AND Other Plants

by TATSUO and KIYOKO ISHIMOTO

CROWN PUBLISHERS, INC., NEW YORK

Library of Congress Catalog Card Number: 66-26185
Printed in the United States of America

Contents

Plants: Undisputed partners of architecture	8
Why shape trees and shrubs?	8
Europeans have been shaping plants for centuries	9
Across Europe in search of topiary	10
The Japanese style of plant shaping	12
Is there an American style of shaping?	13
You have a free hand	14
Shaped plants on a San Francisco hill	16
It's a big bouquet of pompons	17
House and garden work together	18
Streetside gardens—open or closed?	18
The make-up of a garden	19
Placing plants in the garden	20
Entry garden: A general planting selection	20
Entry garden: A specific planting plan	21
Plants have inexhaustible variety	22
Things to keep in mind when selecting your plants	23
Plant shaping	24
Many kinds of shapes to consider	25
Tools	26
When should you prune?	27
How often should you prune?	28
How to develop thick foliage on plants	29
Hedges can be formal or informal	30
Trim often for good hedges	31
Why shrubs need trimming—before and after	32
A young cypress beginning to take shape	34
An aged cypress partly trimmed	35
Bending and tieing	36
Using frames and supports	37
Two-story espalier	37
Pear tree espaliers	38
Sources of ideas	40
Pyramids from Germany and France	41
Three dome shapes found in three countries	42
Natural and topped Italian cypress	44
International two-deckers	46
Trees make a leafy roof	48
Imaginative designs	49
Hedges in France, England, and Portugal	50

Hedges as tunnels and roofs 52
Kew Gardens and Hampton Court Palace, England 55
Topiary at Hampton Court Palace 56
Trees and fountains, France 59
Pillars of cypress, Madrid 60
Flat-top cypresses 63
In Portugal—the art of topiary 64
Topiary with variations 66
Round boxwood garden, Florence 68
Topiary garden in Florence 71
How Italians trim tall trees 72
Creative shaping for hedges 74
Low, shaped boxwood hedges make a design 76
Individuality in neighboring hedges 78
Entrances designed with imagination 79
Square-cut hedges for an entry stair 80
Low hedges for entry stairs 81
Low walls with hedges 82
A hedge arch seems to say "Welcome" 84
Frames for overhead shrubs 87
Stucco and plants for arch and wall 89
Double gates and walls 90
Gardeners' favorite: A pair 92
Combining two different plants can give a pleasing effect 93
Irish yews in pairs 94
Tieing Irish yews to make column shapes 96
Tieing vines to make topiary 99
Shaped plants in containers 100
Trees in boxwood bases 102
Local plants give the best results: Eugenia in San Francisco 104
Many shapes from one species: Eugenia 106
Shapes: Rectangles at entries 108
Variations on the sphere 110
Round shrubs beside steps 112
Variations on Japanese-style plant shaping 114
Shaping Japanese pines 116
Japanese style: The pompon shape 118
Asymmetrical balance 119
Foliage above dancing trunks 120
Three layers against a wall 122
Two-layer holly for accent 123
An eccentric 124
Free form 125

THE ART OF *Shaping*
Shrubs Trees AND *Other Plants*

Plants: Undisputed partners of architecture

One of the things that make our crowded cities and suburbs more habitable and enjoyable is the presence of trees and other plants. As more and more structures and man-made goods are put before us, we become more appreciative of nature. Trees along sidewalks soften the bleakness of the pavement. Architects today are again including planted areas in their designs of city buildings. Plants in containers decorate building entrances that otherwise would be bare and uninviting.

Why shape trees and shrubs?

The garden that goes with today's suburban home often has limited space for plants. In such a case each tree and shrub should have some purpose. As well as being decorative, some will give shade or wind protection, some will act as property dividers, some will guide you along a path, or screen and ornament a building wall. To do their job these plants need help from you. You can help by pruning and shaping to control size, to make them appear clean and healthy, and to create decorative plants and areas. The shaping of plants is simply the cutting of branches and leaves to create some particular form.

All plants have a growth habit, which they will follow unless you do something about it. If you want plants to have a particular shape, formal or informally natural, you have to prune them. Once you have your garden design in mind, you must get to work pruning and training.

In some cases the plant's own growth habit is just what you want. More often you can help matters by eliminating some branches, shortening others, and clipping or shearing foliage.

Some people prefer formal shapes; some people prefer informal or natural shapes. In garden design you can provide both informal and formal plants and make them complement one another. You can design an almost completely formal garden or a garden containing only naturally shaped informal plants.

Topiary in Queluz National Palace, once the residence of the kings of Portugal, near Lisbon.

Europeans have been shaping plants for centuries

The art and practice of shaping trees and shrubs goes back many centuries. In Europe and America it is often called topiary; in Japan it is called *sentei* or *karicomi.*

Some people use the term topiary for plants trained and trimmed in the shape of birds, animals, or various geometric shapes. This kind of plant shaping was started in Europe, and there are still examples to be seen, although it is difficult for tourists to find them. More broadly, the term topiary simply means decorative plant shaping, and a topiary garden is a garden containing shaped plants. A topiary is one example of such a plant.

An old teahouse in Korakuen Gardens in Okayama, Japan, dating from the seventeenth century. House, paving, stones, water, and trees (pruned and kept in miniature) all contribute to this landscape composition.

Across Europe in search of topiary

Making photographs for this book, we traveled through Europe during the months of August, September, and October. In these months the plants on city streets and in residential areas were still green and fresh-looking, especially in Switzerland.

Most of the famous public gardens you see in Europe today were established long before similar gardens got going in the United States. Typically these European gardens are formal with formally shaped plant material, and for centuries they have been pruned to maintain these formal shapes.

The plant collection at the Royal Botanic Gardens at Kew outside London is one of the largest in the world. In Versailles, France, are the world's most celebrated formal gardens. Pyramid-shaped hollies march away from you in straight parallel lines. The Boboli Gardens behind the Pitti Palace in Florence,

This astonishing trimmed hedge looks like a modern store front. It is in the celebrated Boboli Gardens in Florence, Italy.

Italy, are astonishing. From the palace it is impossible to see the extent of the gardens, but if you step out of the palace, you can see trees and shrubs lining both sides of paths for hundreds of yards. These are trimmed to about ten to fifteen feet and cut back while other trees are left in their natural form. And, of course, everywhere are fountains and statues. The column-shaped cypresses in the Palacio Real garden in Madrid are most impressive.

Boxwood topiaries in varied geometrical shapes in the Queluz National Palace in Portugal are celebrated.

For this book we visited and photographed all of these famous gardens and many others in England, Denmark, Sweden, France, Germany, Switzerland, Italy, Spain, and Portugal. We also photographed gardens in the United States, particularly in California, and in Japan. So what you are about to see, really, is an around-the-world look at how gardeners yesterday and gardeners today have been shaping shrubs and trees.

Here is a pair of shaped cypresses at the front entrance of an American house. Each is pruned to a tapered cylinder.

The Japanese style of plant shaping

The shaping of plants in Japan is quite unlike European shaping, probably because the Japanese way of living, Japanese houses, and Japanese plants are all different. Pines are the most popular subjects for plant shaping in Japan. Japanese do wonderful shaping with pines. This pruning achieves an airy result; it follows the natural growth habit of the tree. Another interesting Japanese form is the compact-shaped plant, such as a sheared azalea. Still another favorite garden material is bamboo. Bamboo is used for screens, for boundary planting, and in entries. Dried cut bamboo makes gates and fences, and is used in home interiors.

The public gardens in Japan are really garden museums or garden classrooms. Well-known places such as Katsura Palace in Kyoto, Miyajima near Hiroshima, Suizenji Temple in Kumamoto, and Korakuen in Okayama all contain splendid examples of plant shaping. You will find many examples of the Japanese genius for plant design as you leaf through the pages ahead.

Double pair—boxwood below, euonymus above. The variegated shrubs above are squarish, the boxwoods below are spheres. Usually you would see this design exactly the other way around.

Is there an American style of shaping?

The United States is a continental nation, so our garden climates vary widely. The plants we use depend upon our local climate—how cold it gets in winter, how hot in summer, how much rain, how much clear sunshine. We also live in many different ways—in crowded cities, in small towns, in the country, and in the suburbs. Where gardens have space, we see many trees and shrubs growing naturally; where gardens have less space, shaped trees and shrubs are what can make a splendid garden possible.

Most Americans came from other countries, or their parents or grandparents did. So in the United States, almost every street contains people with varied cultural backgrounds. Each person has brought traditional ideas of garden design with him from France or Italy or Spain or Japan. When you see an American garden, the selection of plants, the garden's design, the shaping of trees or shrubs can sometimes help you recognize which country the garden's owner derives from.

Yet there is certainly an American style. We tend to do things simply. We like a large scale. The photographs you see in this book were made with these American preferences in mind.

You have a free hand

Gardeners in America today shape plants almost any way they like; shapes can be informal and abstract, or literal and geometric. Simple designs using spheres and cubes as their basis are fun to work out. The geometric form does not have to be used literally, of course, but it gives you the starting idea.

The owner of the cypress above told me that he likes to garden, but he admitted that he really does not know one plant from another or what is considered a good shape. But he knows what he likes. He moved to his present address four years ago. At that time this cypress was compact in shape. He decided to clean it up and change its appearance. He had an idea of the shape he wanted, but he was afraid that if he cut the branches all at one time, he might lose the tree. So he cut the branches little by little to achieve this layer-upon-layer abstract form.

Most plants, shrubs, and trees remain healthy if they get regular care, the feeding, water, and pest control they need. And a healthy plant can take almost any kind of reasonable pruning.

Ivy is not usual material for *bonsai,* but here is one. This ivy *bonsai* was started twelve years ago. I cut it back when needed and transplant it when the ivy looks weak. If I start a new one, I shall select small-leaf ivy.

Eugenia is trained as a topiary bird in a container. The idea, frame, tying, and pruning go together to make this topiary. You can make such shapes with many different plants.

Natural-shape marguerite. Good soil, good care, and a good container in the right location make this natural-shape perennial a success.

Shaped plants on a San Francisco hill

This neatly cared for front garden is on a hill in San Francisco and provides a delightful approach to the house. Entering from the street, you walk between two well-pruned hedges which guide you to the door (located in the upper right corner of the picture). On the sides of the stairway, neatly pruned boxwoods in planter boxes are placed in a steplike progression. The espalier and lattice add interest to the garden and decorate the retaining wall. The olive tree, left in its natural form, softens the house and gives a little privacy to the house entrance.

It's a big bouquet of pompons

To achieve the airy Japanese pompon effect, follow the natural form of the tree, keeping the strong branches intact. Trim the leaves into interesting clusters with open spaces between them.

On this tall olive tree, the ends of the branches are pruned to form pompons. The open foliage lets light into the planted area below, and the tree becomes a pruner's work of art. With a show-stopper like this, you want to keep adjacent planting quietly pruned and out of visual competition.

House and garden work together

It is the American dream to live in a good house with a good garden in a good neighborhood. Some people prefer to have their homes on a steep hillside with a view and less usable garden area; others like a home on a level lot with a good deal of usable garden space. Yet most Americans seem to pay more attention to choosing a neighborhood and a house than they do to choosing a lot that will make an interesting garden or a house that already has an interesting garden. If you give them equal attention, your garden and your house interior can work together in perfect relationship and balance. But if you think of the garden as secondary, if you neglect it, what an opportunity you miss.

Streetside gardens—open or closed?

In every city you see two approaches to the residential streetside garden. One approach provides privacy. This is accomplished with fencing, walls, or hedges. The other type is the opposite. Here the gardener wants light, a feeling of openness. He uses lawn or clear space with low-growing plants. His purpose is to set off the house and to provide a garden entry that invites one in.

The make-up of a garden

Houses are placed on lots in many different ways. This is owing to the size of the lot and its general shape, the size of the house, and the contour of the land. The available garden area will be the result of these factors. Nevertheless, most gardens have fairly standard features or parts: an entry, various planted areas, perhaps a play-space for the children, pathways, some sort of terrace or other outdoor sitting area.

Here is an example of a garden floor plan. On the street side there is a lawn and a sidewalk, a path to the house entrance and one to the side entrance. The path connecting the street and the main entrance is the one most home owners prefer to have paved in order to welcome guests and to keep the house clean. In this example, the paths lead quite directly to both entrances. Along the front path is the entry garden. A tall fence or hedge on the property line will give much privacy to front windows. If you wish to be able to look out of the windows, a lawn or low ground cover and low shrubs will make an equally attractive entry garden.

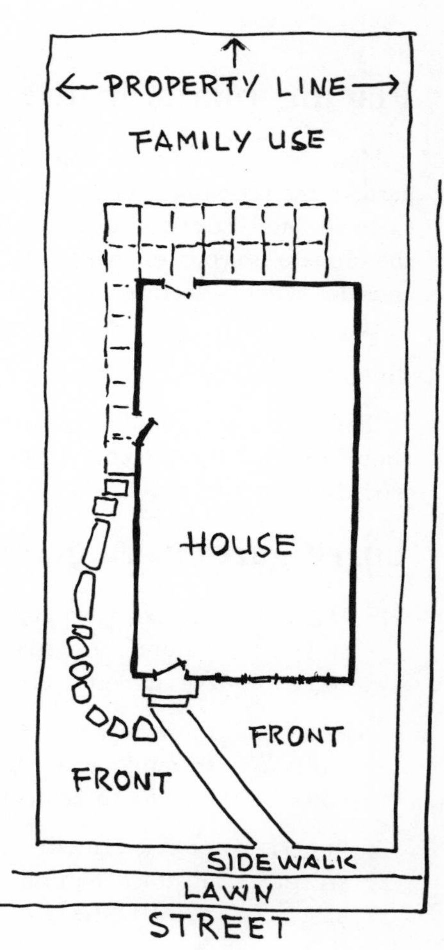

Usually, the large private garden area in back of a house is for family use. Here garden design can be more relaxed than in front. The front garden is more formal because it faces the public world. Both sides of the house have less space, just paths to connect front and back areas. Naturally a less decorative garden design is usual here.

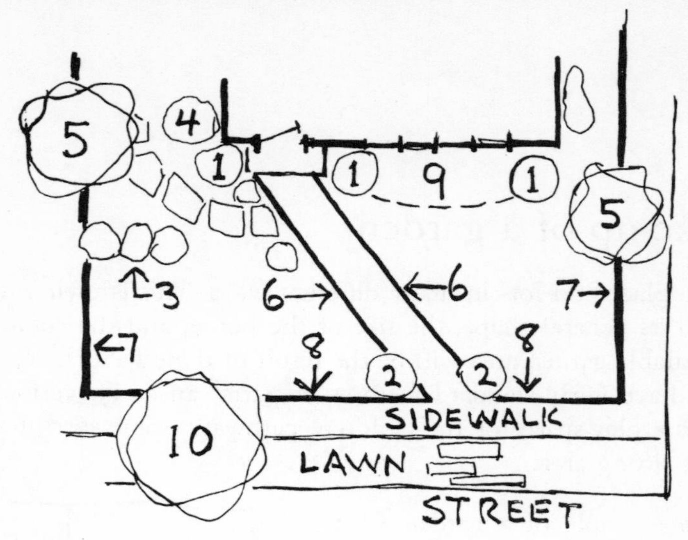

Placing plants in the garden

Your garden planting plan depends on so many variables—the size of your garden, the relationship between the garden and the house, your neighbors, the sidewalk and street, the street gradient and the lot gradient, your views, the climate of your town and the climate of your lot. All these are things to consider when selecting plants.

The right placement of the right plants is probably the most important thing the garden maker does.

The above is a simple garden plan for the front of a house. The numbers show some of the possible types of plant material that can be used. Which would be your selection?

Entry garden: A general planting selection

1. PLANTS: cypress, yew, eugenia, camellia, variegated shrubs
   SHAPE: natural, rectangular, columnar, oval, pompon
   SIZE: two to eight feet

2. PLANTS: boxwood, cypress, yew, juniper, holly
   SHAPE: rectangular, round, natural, abstract
   SIZE: one to three feet

3. PLANTS: privet, camellia, nandina, bamboo
   SHAPE: abstract, natural, hedge, screen
   SIZE: three to six feet

4. PLANTS: privet, camellia, mirror plant, rose, orange, lemon, fuchsia
   SHAPE: rectangular, natural, loose screen
   SIZE: seven inches to eight feet

5. PLANTS: olive, flowering trees, holly
   SHAPE: natural, umbrella shape
   SIZE: seven to ten feet

6. PLANTS: boxwood, flower beds, lawn extending to the edge
   SHAPE: continuous hedge, rounded line, squarish line, flower beds, lawn to the edge
   SIZE: four to eight inches

7. PLANTS: privet, boxwood, cypress, juniper, cotoneaster, mirror plant
   SHAPE: straight top or designed continuous hedge
   SIZE: five inches to eight feet

8. same as 7

9. PLANTS: azalea, juniper, flower beds
   SHAPE: ground cover effect
   SIZE: low

10. PLANTS: tree (low branches should allow passage beneath them), olive, waxed leaf privet, bay tree, crataegus (hawthorn), acacia
    SHAPE: natural, trimmed shape, umbrella shape, standard
    SIZE: tall

Entry garden: A specific planting plan

(This one is for the climate of northern California. For much of America you would substitute hardy trees and shrubs for such plants as olive and nandina.)

1. cypress, pompon, seven feet
2. holly, round, eighteen inches
3. nandina, natural, four feet
4. camellia, natural, three feet wide, six feet tall
5. olive, ten feet, umbrella shape on left, natural on right
6. boxwood hedge, six inches
7. privet, six feet on left, eight feet on right
8. boxwood, eight inches
9. azalea, low
10. acacia, branches starting at six feet from ground, trimmed shape

Low-growing juniper below. Young yew will grow through in a column shape.

Grown tree (mirror plant). It can be trained either natural form or pompon shape.

Plants have inexhaustible variety

All plants have their own characteristics of growing, fast or slow, tall or short, thin or wide; of leaf, size, color, and texture in immense variety. And plants of the same type never grow in exactly the same way.

There is a multitude of plants for you to choose from in working out your garden design. Because of soil and climate factors, it is best to select your plants at a local nursery. It will carry plants that are known to do well in your area.

For a compact shape in the garden, both the needle-bearing conifers and broad-leafed evergreen shrubs are suitable, because they have foliage all the year round and you can also train and shape them into almost any formal or natural form you desire.

Deciduous trees are mostly trained along their natural forms, and usually you will let them grow tall.

This is an example of how a tree grows and takes a shape. The tip of a cypress is bent and tied to a post to create a curved shape. Notice the way in which the branches are growing up. Almost all plants grow toward the sun or light.

Things to keep in mind when selecting your plants

Trees and shrubs are unlike flowers; you do not replace them every year or even every few years. Once you select it and plant it, your tree or shrub will stay for many years. Therefore, you should be very careful when making your selection.

Naturally, you will select plants you like. You should know the growing habits of the plants you have selected—how fast they grow, their future size, and their natural forms—and they should harmonize with the house and the surrounding plants.

When you begin your garden, you will most likely be working with small plants, so it is important to remember how much space the plants will need in the future. You must be careful not to plant them too close to other plants or too close to a wall, unless it is your plan to do so. Many gardens become severely crowded as the plants grow.

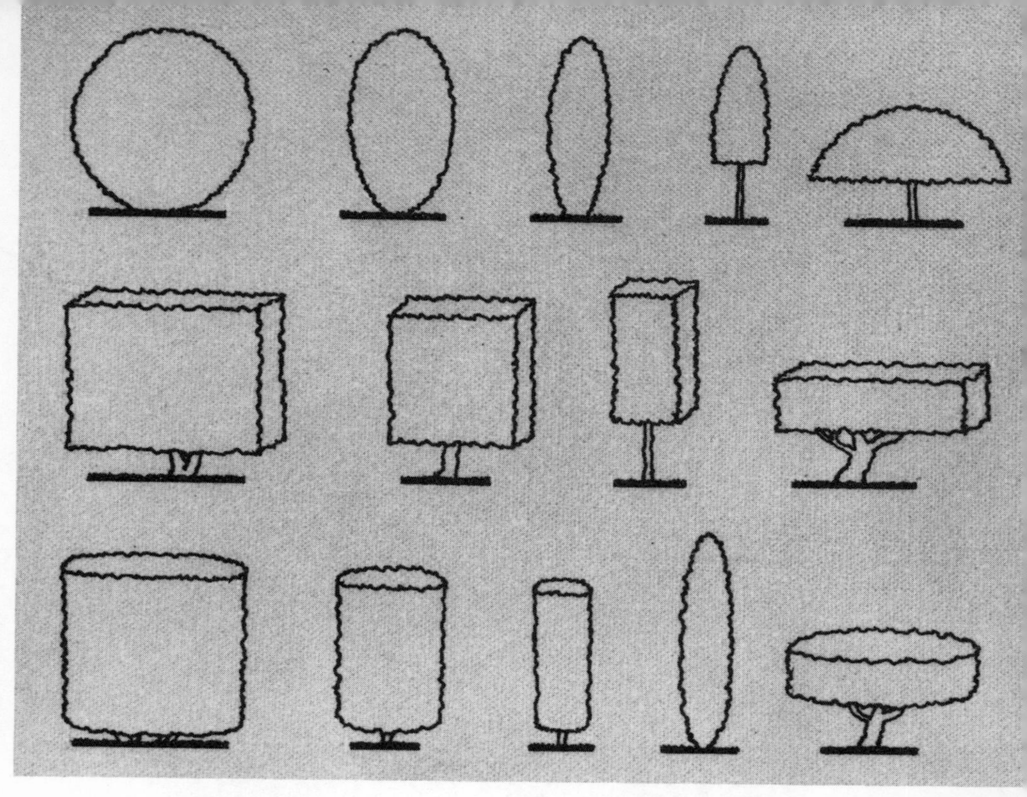

European shaping: Here are fourteen typical geometric forms used in European topiary and also long used in America.

Plant shaping

In this book we are using the term shaping to mean the training and pruning of plants into some desired form.

Of course, established hedges and shrubs are easiest to cut, because the form is already there to follow.

Basic symmetrical shapes for plants are globes and cubes and many variations on these two forms. Other basic forms are the column, the pyramid, and the cone. All are much used in European topiary.

The Japanese style allows the natural form to remain. Pruning emphasizes and enhances the various shapes by opening up the spaces between the branches and creating new spaces. What we call do-it-yourself shape is simply an original form. The more successful ones are well balanced either symmetrically or asymmetrically.

Topiary shaping of trees and shrubs into animal, bird, or geometric shapes can be imaginative and humorous.

Natural and Japanese: These forms all follow the plants' natural growth habit, but how imagination enters the picture.

To espalier is to train plants two-dimensionally (usually against a wall) to follow trellises or frames that have certain patterns. Espaliers typically are both formal and symmetrical, but they do not have to be.

Many kinds of shapes to consider

The desirable garden has a variety of plants in a variety of shapes and sizes. This variety can include natural trees, some Japanese-shaped types, and some compact-shaped shrubs, all within a range of sizes. You can establish a harmonious setting with a group of similarly shaped trees interspersed with a few other forms for variety.

In an established garden, if it is to look well, shapes and sizes of trees and shrubs must be under control. But this certainly does not mean the plants all need to be perfect globes, cubes, or columns. It simply means the plants must be in good relationship to each other, to the area of the garden, and to the house.

Pruning shears will enable you to do fine pruning on branches and stems without cutting the leaves.

Lopping shears cut branches.

Hedge shears are used for making flat surfaces, as they will trim both leaves and branches.

Electric shears are used for the same purpose as hedg shears, but they are easier and faster. When you ar trimming hedges with electric shears, it is easiest t trim upward.

Tools

You need very little equipment for pruning and shaping. The basic equipment for shaping your trees and shrubs and trimming your hedges consists of pruning shears, lopping shears, and hedge shears. Electric shears are a timesaver. A pruning saw is necessary if you will be cutting thick branches or trunks.

I have noticed that in Europe, America, and Japan, gardeners use quite similar tools for pruning.

In pruning, as in so many crafts, it pays to buy good tools and to care for them. Shears that are strong and sharp are a great pleasure.

When should you prune?

Most plants can take some trimming at any season of the year. But all plants, even the tolerant conifers, have one season that is best for pruning. This season will vary somewhat by climate. It will be wise for you to discuss pruning timing with your local nurseryman and with experienced gardeners living near you.

Here is a general guide to pruning timing.

Conifers: Early spring before new growth starts is the best time. Late summer and fall are good times to trim and thin.

Deciduous trees and shrubs: When they are out of leaf and dormant is the best pruning time. Never prune in spring, but trimming and thinning are quite all right in late summer and fall.

Broadleaf evergreens: Late winter and early spring are the best pruning times, late summer and fall best for trimming and thinning.

Flowering fruit trees: The time to prune is immediately after the blossom.

Before you prune any plant, it is wise to study the future effects. Once you cut, you cannot put the branches back.

Don't.

Do.

Once in a while shrubs need to be cleaned of dead branches. This aged euonymus was photographed on August 16, 1965.

Lopping shears and pruning shears are used to cl up unwanted or dead branches and at the same ti make more spaces between the branches while s keeping the original contour form.

How often should you prune?

The frequency with which you should prune most plants depends on the plants themselves and the climate in which you live, and on this point too local nurserymen give the best advice.

Very severe shapes need to be pruned often. If you want to keep them cleanly defined, prune or trim new growth as soon as it comes out.

ame shrubs on April 3, 1966, about seven and a half onths later. More leaves have grown, and it needs little pruning.

Same shrub after being pruned with pruning shears. This time more leaves are left to make the pompon look.

How to develop thick foliage on plants

Most shrubs will produce more branches to replace branches that have been pruned. What was one branch becomes two or three. At the next pruning these become six or more, and so on. For this reason when you want compact foliage on certain branches, prune accordingly.

This neglected hedge needs care badly.

Hedges can be formal or informal

Hedges are ideal for privacy and they are useful as property dividers. Most often you see them at the edge of the lot or on the lot line.

The height can be anything from a foot up to eight feet, or even higher, depending on the owner's choice. The width too may vary from a few inches to twenty inches or more.

Generally a number of shrubs of the same kind are planted close together in a row to create a hedge. Established hedges are most often trimmed neatly with flat sides and square edges, but sometimes the edges are trimmed round for smoothness. The top edge can be straight, wavy, or uneven. Or some additional ornamental forms can be placed on the top. Or the hedge can be quite informal, pruned only to keep it within bounds, but with no straight sides.

The end of a hedge at a gate or an entrance can be made higher than the rest. You can add pillars or some decorative shapes to the top of it, or you can shape it to create a canopy or arch effect.

Above: A once neglected hedge newly pruned. *Below:* A properly cared-for hedge.

Trim often for good hedges

This principle applies to most hedges. So when you start a hedge, do not wait for the shrubs to reach the height you want, or you will probably get a thin, weak-looking hedge. If you want a five-foot hedge, wait until the shrubs grow to three feet, then trim them back half way; then wait until the shrubs grow another three feet and trim half of the new part. This will force branching and also produce strong trunks. Repeat this procedure until you have got the height you want. After the hedge has been established, simply trim to control the size and shape, two to four times a year, depending on species and climate.

August 16, 1965, this wax leafed privet appeared like this before being cleaned.

The shaping idea is a cube. First trimming shears w
used to get the general shape.

Why shrubs need trimming—before and after

This wax leafed privet has been well established and so it can take lots of pruning. With such a plant you can use any tools you like to make the final shape. I used pruning, hedge, and lopping shears. Before taking the last picture I used hedge shears, because I can work faster with them. As you see, the final result is about the same as if I had used pruning shears.

Old branches and leaves have been removed with lopping and pruning shears. Very few leaves are left on the tree. Do not worry; it will not die. In fact this rough treatment is good for the tree. Now it looks fresh and healthy.

April 2, 1966, seven and a half months later, the tree looked as it does in this picture. I could make it either its original shape or pompon style and decided to make it pompon style.

Pruned again, this time mainly using hedge shears, because they are easier and faster.

A young cypress beginning to take shape

The lower part of this young cypress is shaped. The top part still remains in its natural form. The next step will be another similar shape on top of the already established form, and probably later, one more form. The shape will then be controlled, because the area for planting is limited.

An aged cypress partly trimmed

This large cypress is trimmed at the base and in its natural form above. The reason for this trimming is to leave the sidewalk clear. A large woody plant like this can be controlled by being trimmed during its early growth, and so kept in scale with its surroundings.

Branches tied to wires attached to hooks fastened to the wall (see end of branches).

Bending and tieing

You can also sometimes bend branches and tie them to create shape and line. I prefer to use rope or plastic line, as wire tends to cut into bark and will damage a tree if not removed in time.

In the spring, when trees start growing again, their branches are tender and flexible and are easy to bend. Spring, therefore, is the best time to do bending.

When you work with a tree, you have to be gentle and careful in order to avoid breaking the branches.

A wooden crosspiece and wires. The frame is some inches away from the wall, allowing air to circulate.

Using frames and supports

When you want your plants to arch over an open space or to make an espalier, you will usually need to give them support. A frame should be provided to guide new growth into the desired shape. Frames can be made of steel, pipe, branches, or light lumber, and you can sometimes use wire.

Two-story espalier

An espalier is a tree or shrub trained, usually against a wall, to create a two-dimensional effect. You can also do an espalier in the open garden (not against a wall), but your plants will need a frame to follow. Tie the branches you want to keep to a wood-and-wire frame and prune unwanted branches. Some branches will need a little bending. The pear espalier at the top of the page was photographed at the Botanic Gardens in Bern, Switzerland.

Pear tree espaliers

Here in Malmo, Sweden, you see pear trees trained as espaliers against a building wall. Notice how the plant trainer has made the branches avoid the windows. Branches are tied to metal hooks in the brick wall and to strips of wood. If you look at them not as trees but as abstract patterns, the effects are very attractive.

Above is the corner view of the espalier on the previous page. The branches have all been trained to turn the corner and a wooden frame is used for support, because the trunk is far on the other side.

On the right are two more pictures of espalier-trained pear trees.

Sources of ideas

You can collect ideas for plant shapes and garden design in many places: garden magazines, books, newspapers, and your own observations on walks and travels. Or perhaps you will want to work out an original design of your own.

Our approach to the matter of how to shape trees and shrubs is similar to that we used in *The Art of the Japanese Garden* and *The Japanese House,* for which we took trips to Japan in search of ideas. For this book we have prowled through Europe from the Baltic to the Mediterranean. We photographed a great many plant forms in European gardens, rarely seen here in the United States. For example, on these two pages you see large and small pyramid-shaped trees. Surely you can duplicate the small ones in your garden. Although the large gardens we show are not on a residential scale, the important thing always is the idea, not the size. Shapes can easily be adapted to the smallest garden.

Pyramids from Germany and France

Left: These pyramid-shaped boxwoods in back of an office building in Munich, Germany, are only twenty-four inches high. Grouped in a corner area, they make a pleasant sight from inside the offices and from this angle, too.

Above: The famous Versailles gardens outside Paris cover about two hundred and fifty acres and are most formal. One of the fascinating plant displays is this parade of seven-foot pyramid-shaped hollies, a trim and proper honor guard for the palace. The trees you see in the background are surrounded by colorful flowers. All are pruned to cones.

Three dome shapes found in three countries

The dome shape can be used in a variety of ways. These pictures, taken in Italy, Japan, and the United States, show how the shape is adapted to different situations.

Above: Rounded trees are intermixed with the short hedge in a masonry planter along a street in Pistoia, Italy. The shape of the hedge is already well established. All that it needs is a bit of pruning.

The right name for single-stemmed pruned trees like these is "standard." These standards are privets and cotoneasters.

This tall pruned bay tree grows beside a sidewalk in residential San Francisco. The owner has trimmed his tree to a standard that will not reach out to bother passing pedestrians.

These rounded azaleas are in the entrance area of the Meiji Shrine in Tokyo. The shapes start immediately from the ground. Such squashed, ground-hugging hemispheres are quite characteristic of the Japanese style.

Natural and topped Italian cypress

The natural habit of the Italian cypress is to grow straight up, as tall and almost as slim as a telephone pole. Planted to keynote a large landscaped area, it can be really dramatic.

We took this photograph at a nursery in Pistoia, Italy. These tall cypresses are planted in wooden containers and supported by poles. If you buy three for your villa, the nurseryman will bring them to you in their boxes.

Here is a cypress ballet. These are trimmed cypresses on stage behind a neat low hedge. It is the Palacio Real garden in Madrid.

Topped Irish yews on each side of an entrance. The low-cut boxwood hedges just make the yews more important.

Italian cypresses and Irish yews are very decorative when topped and trimmed to make column shapes. These two trees are among the most popular in both European and American formal gardens. Often you see this shape used in pairs to flank a residential entrance.

Variegated holly five feet tall, France.

Variegated holly three feet tall, France.

Variegated euonymus six feet tall, Barcelona, Spain.

Privet four feet tall, Amsterdam, Netherlands.

International two-deckers

These two pages present various shrubs shaped in two parts photographed in Europe and America. The pictures were taken beside a railroad station, in a park, beside a government building, and in private gardens.

Obviously the gardeners and caretakers of these plants take pride in their work. These double-deck plants require more time and care than they would if they had been left to grow naturally. But the work must be worth it. What fun to come home, look, and say to yourself, "That's mine."

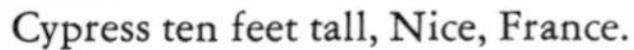

Cypress ten feet tall, Nice, France.

Boxwood one and one-half feet tall, San Francisco.

A double-decked design is created from one plant or from two plants shaped into one. What you need is a little open space about the middle.

Top left: Eugenias are planted between two houses to serve as a screen.

Top right: At a gasoline station in Italy, a single privet shaped like two balloons. Is it designed to attract business?

Lower left: A cypress hedge with an ornamental shape on top. The cypress blends neatly with the wooden fence.

Lower right: It looks like two, but you are really seeing just one boxwood in a planter. Small, shaped plants such as this do nicely in containers.

Trees make a leafy roof

Among Italian cities Sorrento is known both for its climate and for its songs. A short distance from Naples, the city is located on a hill overlooking the sea. The district is famous for its oranges, lemons, and olives. In Sorrento we saw this unusual shade shelter made of pruned and trained trees. Under the cool shade of the plant roof, horses and carriages await the tourists.

Imaginative designs

A low, shaped azalea at the side of a path in Japan. The azalea is not planted in the water, but half of it gracefully leans over it. This must be especially beautiful in blossom time.

This is one of the most unusually shaped shrubs we have seen. It is really the terminus of a broad and lofty hedge planting. It is in back of the Palazzo Pitti, in the beautiful Boboli Gardens, Florence, Italy.

Untrimmed cypresses stand above the pruned hedges. La Turbie, ten miles from Nice, southern France.

Hedges in France, England, and Portugal

Hedges are most often used to separate spaces or as property dividers, because their structure make them ideally suited to these purposes. But you can do many other things with hedges. Notice that all three hedges shown here have other plants in relation to them.

Above: Cypress hedges at the sides of steps suggest direction and add more interest to the steps.

Here one tall hedge is a divider for the property, another on the left is a divider for the garden. This arrangement also makes the driveway between the two hedges less noticeable. London, England.

The hedge here defines the place of the entry walk. The hedge and the low plant on the right together create the effect of a gate. Lisbon, Portugal.

Hedges as tunnels and roofs

These photographs were made in Boboli Gardens in Florence, Italy. They show a most fanciful type of shaping. The idea is to cut out a tunnel or aperture or to create an overhang. It is done on a large scale, as you can see by comparing the size of the figure in the picture above to that of the tunnel.

Above: This cut-in niche is actually tunneled completely through the hedge. It makes a handsome background for the statue and of course draws attention to this spot in the long green wall.

Right: This corner of the hedge is an overhang. It shows how deep some of the cut-ins can go.

Shaped Irish yews before Kew Palace in Kew Gardens. This planting is designed to be enjoyed from the palace windows above.

Close-up of shaped Irish yews in Kew Gardens. They stand above low-growing plants in rectangular planted areas, both set into a green lawn.

Pointed umbrella- or cone-shaped hollies in the gardens at Hampton Court Palace. This arrangement of trees makes a delightful shady area in which summer visitors can stroll and relax.

Kew Gardens and Hampton Court Palace, England

If you ask a hotel clerk, a policeman, or a taxi driver in London where you can go to see an interesting garden, he most likely will tell you to go to Kew Gardens and Hampton Court Palace. The Royal Botanic Gardens at Kew, thirty minutes by subway or one and a half hours by Thames boat upriver from central London, covers about three hundred acres and is the world's best-known botanic garden. There are countless species of trees, shrubs, flowers, and succulent plants, as well as statuary, tropical and temperate greenhouses, and even Chinese Guardian Lions and a Pagoda.

Hampton Court Palace is just outside London. It is easy to reach, and the palace and gardens are surprisingly vast and impressive. The many large, shaped hollies in rows pictured above are famous. Another interesting garden area near the palace is the Pond Garden pictured on the following pages.

Topiary at Hampton Court Palace

This sunken garden has a pond as its main attraction. From the pond, paths lead to each side of the rectangular area. Lawn, shaped shrubs, varied flower beds, and statues fill the colorful and formal garden design. From this view you see the great rectangular cypress at the far end. Part of this cypress has been trimmed and cut out to make a shelter for the statue.

This view is from the side of the garden. The cone-shaped yews are about four feet tall, and the abstract-shaped boxwoods are about twenty inches high. Compare this view with the photograph on the opposite page.

Versailles, France. A band of three-inch-high dwarf boxwood appears to pass through a twenty-inch-high boxwood dome. The dwarf boxwood establishes a border line. The dome is there simply to add interest.

These two shaped cypresses in the gardens of the Louvre, Paris, have double hedges for decoration and protection. Both hedges surround the trees entirely. You will notice the low wire barrier along the edge of the lawn to keep people off the grass.

Trees and fountains, France

In Paris, every visitor to the Eiffel Tower should cross the bridge to walk through the Jardins du Trocadero. There he will see the shaped cypress pictured here. They make a beautiful contrast to the white spray of the fountains. These shapes are much like those of trees you see at Versailles.

Pillars of cypress, Madrid

Madrid is a fascinating city for any gardener to visit. There are so many historic buildings, parks, statues, fountains, and tree-lined streets. The gardens have been well maintained and so have the street trees. One of the most noticeable tree forms in Madrid is the topped cypress pictured here. This column shape seems to be popular throughout the world.

This formal garden is simply the side yard of the formidable Palacio Real in Madrid. The garden is quite severe in design, and the column-shaped cypresses seem especially appropriate because they echo the shape and line of the marble columns of the palace. The low, neatly pruned plants are boxwoods.

Certain things are much the same in every country. In Europe, in the Orient, in America, where city hall or main plaza is to be found, there are always pigeons. In the country there is laundry hanging outside the houses. In public gardens workmen are always digging something up and making repairs. If you look closely, you will see that the Royal Palace garden is being dug up for repairs.

Flat-top cypresses

These photographs give us a closer look at the Palacio Real garden. The above picture was photographed looking down in order to let us see the elaborate and formal design of the boxwoods. And, of course, the dark-green topped cypresses at the corners make it all the more dramatic.

The pictures on the opposite page show the even lines and height of the hedges, the precise spacing and shaping of the cypresses. What patience, planning, and pruning skill it took to create these handsome sculptured shapes made of living materials.

A large dome and a top-pointed cylinder topiary, Queluz National Palace.

In Portugal—the art of topiary

Queluz National Palace is located in a suburb of Lisbon. Inside the palace you can see antique furniture, paintings, historical mementoes. Outside in the garden you will see antique topiaries, boxwoods shaped in squares, geometrical figures, tall and short, unusually shaped plants individually and in groups.

The Queluz National Palace garden is full of ideas for you to take home and try out. For instance, if you have a round plant, why not try giving it a pointed top?

Topiary group around a pond. Some are almost mosque-shaped.

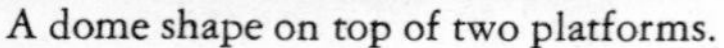

A dome shape on top of two platforms.

A hemisphere shape above platform and hedge.

Topiary with variations

On these two pages you see a few of the many topiaries in the Queluz garden. The shapes may at first appear to be the same, but each form has its own individuality. The tops range in shape from spires to domes. The lower portions maintain balance and serve as bases or platforms.

Compact-growing plants are well suited to formal shapes. This European shaping concept is completely different from the open, natural look of the Japanese style.

Half-oval shape with double base.

Half-oval shape on triple base.

Three-sided cone shape pointed at top.

Four-sided cone shape pointed at top on a double sculptured base.

Round boxwood garden, Florence

Florence, in Italy, is certainly one of the most beautiful cities in Europe. Here, in the private garden of Mrs. Piera Stross, we see many kinds of topiary. During certain days each spring, tourists are invited to visit and admire this garden.

In one area there are groups of similar round boxwoods. They are interesting to view from different angles. On these pages there are three views of the same living spheres, sitting there for all the world like so many giant leafy soccer balls.

Topiary garden in Florence

You need a bit of imagination to recognize what these topiary creations represent. Although the forms are fully developed, the correct word to explain the shapes is "abstract." Unfortunately, we did not visit this garden during quite the right season, so some of the plants had not yet been trimmed. Even so, you can get the idea.

How Italians trim tall trees

You might find this oversized ladder a bit large around your home, but it is what gardeners use in Florence, Italy, to shape tall trees. The size and weight of this stepladder requires four men to move it from one place to another. With it a man can work on very tall trees and hedges.

To keep a straight edge, these gardeners use two strings as guides. Notice that near the top of the ladder a string hangs perpendicular to the ground. Another string is positioned along the base of the trees about ten inches above the ground. These strings are only guides; skill is still required to form a good edge. You may find this procedure helpful even though you are working with a one-man ladder on shorter hedges.

Neatly trimmed hedges on the lot line enclose the entire front garden. On the neighbor's side the hedge is higher for the sake of privacy. There are two entrances, one at the side of the garage and the other on the street, but they are hardly noticeable.

Creative shaping for hedges

Because people's tastes, ideas, needs, and talents differ so much, we see all kinds and shapes of hedges. Above and on the facing page, you see three quite differently shaped hedges. Two things they all have in common are the owner's desire to have privacy and define his property line.

Here a curved stucco wall is modified by a hedge planted on the garden side. The curved top of the wall is filled with hedge and trimmed straight. This looks like a European arrangement, but the picture was taken in San Francisco.

This cypress masterpiece was shaped partly to provide privacy by hiding the window, partly as a property divider and fence, and partly as a work of art. Such a treasure as this, I am afraid, cannot be created overnight.

Low, shaped boxwood hedges make a design

This approach to garden design with its use of a low hedge is very popular in Europe. Well-trimmed boxwoods serve as both a divider and an enclosure for colorful flower beds.

Few Americans would want to attempt such a design on this scale. But simplified, the idea simply is to use hedge planting to establish a basic garden design.

On both side of an entrance, low trimmed boxwood hedges divide planted areas and sidewalk. The rounded plants inside the hedges add interest and vertical scale.

Here boxwoods planted in the center of a lawn on a corner lot are trimmed low. The design follows the line of the curved sidewalk. The azalea adds color and interest to the design.

The square plants to the left of the gate are privets, and those to the right are cypress. The gate belongs to the house on the left.

Individuality in neighboring hedges

Everyone likes to have his house and garden express his personality.

The picture above shows how two neighbors shaped their hedges to suit their own taste. This example happens to be in Lisbon, but you can find similar examples on thousands of streets in the United States.

Here two shrubs of different varieties, the leaves of one dark green and those of the other variegated, are mingled in the same hedge. This mingling makes an interesting design. At the end of the hedge is a shape that looks like an old-fashioned jar-top.

The hedge flanks a path leading to steps and entrance door. It is eye-catching and also gives privacy, screening the house from the next property.

Entrances designed with imagination

A hedge marking out an entrance way usually begins at the sidewalk and continues along the side of the path to the steps. Not much more effort is needed to make your hedge distinctive. You can prune it and add ornamental shapes, or work out an original design. Such a design can make the care of your hedge much more enjoyable.

Square-cut hedges for an entry stair

A house built on a hill usually has steps leading to the entrance from the sidewalk. There are several ways in which you can make these steps more inviting. One way is to have flanking hedges. Above is an interesting example of such a hedge.

Privets have been planted as hedges on each side of the steps and given a rectangular trim. On the step side the plants seem the same height, but notice the driveway side: the plants on this side are taller than those on the lawn.

Low hedges for entry stairs

Here are more examples of hedges used to flank stairs. The settings are neat and well maintained, and have a less formal effect than the arrangement in the previous picture.

The plants on both sides of the steps in the picture below are low-growing cotoneasters. The high hedges at the top of the steps are privets.

Left alone, a low cotoneaster will grow into a sprawling shape. Cut back, a cotoneaster will form the kind of shape pictured here.

These steps are lined with neatly trimmed boxwoods shaped into rectangles with a globe at each end.

A hedge like a series of waves on top of a low brick wall in a London suburb.

Low walls with hedges

A hedge combined with a wall can be very simple in construction, but endless variety is possible. The simplest way to obtain individuality is to change the appearance of the top of the hedge. If you are planning a hedge and wall, here are some suggestions.

If you have a wall with a straight top, make the hedge top uneven; if you have an uneven wall, use the hedge to straighten it out. You can even add some ornamental form on top, as shown in the lower picture on opposite page (although I would like this idea better if the cone and ball shapes were either closer together or larger).

A hedge used to establish a level line on top of an uneven brick wall in a London suburb.

A stucco wall with a steel fence above it and a hedge planted inside it. The conical and ball-shaped cypress rising above the hedge are unusual adornments. Pistoia, Italy.

A hedge arch seems to say "Welcome"

Fences for privacy and gates for entrance—these are universal elements in garden design. You can use lumber or masonry for your fences and gates; you also can use plant materials, or both in combination. The plant materials are the important thing in the pictures on these two pages.

Throughout Europe we found the hedge arch to be a favorite of garden designers. It was frequently used both in parks and in residential gardens as an entrance way. Pictured above is a hedge arch we saw in Malmo, Sweden. The hedge arches over with no change in width to create an inviting garden entrance.

Overhead plants need frames to support and maintain their shape.

In a residential area in London, England, we photographed a hedge with a leafy arch that was quite similar to the one we saw in Sweden.

This fence uses four materials: stone and brick below, then vertical boards, then clipped hedge on top. A wooden fence would have been simpler and would have afforded equal privacy, but how much nicer it is when plants are used as well as building materials and when the owner takes the pains to shape his plants.

Inside this wooden gate you see a sort of canopy over the path formed by plants. The thick hedge on the right is continued along the wooden fence.

Man's help is needed both in the creation of overhead hedges and in their maintenance. Plants cannot put on a performance such as you see in this picture all on their own. Many conifers can make living archways, and some broad-leafed evergreens also. Overhead plants need a frame to hold the branches. Bend the branches and tie them to the frame. While creating the shape, prune continually. The shape of hedge arches is usually harmonized with the rest of the hedge and its surroundings.

The arch pictured here is made of cypress; the shape is semicylindrical. This arch is well established now and needs only occasional pruning. It was photographed in a residential area in Lisbon, Portugal.

This iron arch frame supports cypress. Nice, France.

A wooden arch frame for pittosporums to follow. San Francisco.

Frames for overhead shrubs

To create an arched hedge you need a frame for the branches to follow. You then tie the branches to the frame. Sometimes they have to be bent, and some pruning will also be necessary.

You can use many different materials for the frame. Wood, steel, pipe, wire, and dried branches are the most common.

This simple iron arch frame is held by square masonry posts. The privets have not yet grown enough to complete the arch.

This tunnel is in the Giardino di Boboli in Florence, Italy. Here slim trees have been planted in a row on each side of a path. The tips of the trees have been bent, entwined, and tied with wire and rope to the trees on the opposite side. Where the branches are not yet long enough, dried branches of this species that look alive have been used to complete the arch and create a shady tunnel over the path. For evergreen arches, dried natural branches are often more suitable and harmonious than stiff lumber or metal.

The top of the arch is semicylindrical and higher than the rectangular sections that join the arch to the rest of the hedge. The sidewalk is made of small tiles.

Stucco and plants for arch and wall

Here is a stucco wall and a gate with harmoniously shaped shrubs on top. Notice the width and thickness of the shrubs. The arch is so thick that passing beneath it feels like walking through a tunnel. As you can see, the privet has been pruned to echo the shape of the stucco wall and gate.

Double gates and walls

Left: On the street side, stucco, stones, and iron make a gate and wall. Within the garden, shaped cypress make another gate and wall.

A column-shaped cypress has been planted on each side of the gate and the two have been connected at the top to form an arch. The cypress ball on top of the arch is just a bit of whimsy.

Below: The top of a gate is covered by variegated ivy, and on both sides of it are cypress in shapes that remind one of the bearskin caps worn by the Guards in London.

Both these gates were photographed in Nice, France.

This is the main entrance; over it eugenia branches make an arch. The stone wall provides a curved base for a eugenia tree hedge, which resembles a vine. San Francisco.

This is a side entrance; eugenias have grown over the gate and formed a canopy.

Gardeners' favorite: A pair

Many home owners like to convey a feeling of balance on an entrance path. This balance is commonly achieved by two plants, both of the same species, placed one on each side of a path and making a pair.

Here is a handsome variation on this idea. Two large mirror plants stand one on each side of an entrance. The trunks are interestingly different, but the shape of the foliage is so well judged that the complete plant composition seems in balance.

Where mirror plants grow vigorously, they need frequent pruning to keep them from spreading and getting out of hand.

A mirror plant and a cypress planted close together have been shaped as if they were one tree. But the mirror plant grows faster, so it needs more frequent trimming.

With a little imagination you can create many remarkable shapes. Here eugenias have been woven to form a cheerful leafy arch.

Combining two different plants can give a pleasing effect

Pairs of plants can be combined in several different ways. It is fun to repeat the same shape in two different plants, to give a pair of the same species different shapes, and to shape two plants as one. For a harmonious effect, use similar plants, but for surprise try combining two different textures or colors of foliage.

Here you see two identically shaped cypresses, one on each side of a wire fence, and also shaped pittosporum crassifolium planted along the fence to form a hedge.

Irish yews in pairs

In these pictures Irish yews are planted in pairs in entrance areas. You see three different shapes used in three different places, but in each case the idea is to accentuate the entrance way.

The natural habit of Italian cypress is to grow slim and tall. If you would like Irish yews to have the same appearance as Italian cypress, then the Irish yews need help from you.

The yews in the pictures on this page and on the opposite page were at one time tied at the top and the side to encourage a compact shape.

Here is an example of Irish yews planted as a rather formal pair. Yews take well to this tall, slim shape.

These Irish yews were planted forty-two years ago one on each side of an entry path. They are now old and plump but perfectly healthy.

A pair of Irish yews one on each side of a garden gate. The tops have been cut down level with the top of the garden wall.

Tieing Irish yews to make column shapes

If you want Irish yews to grow in a tall, slim, column shape, you must tie them at the side and top. Along with pruning, this will keep them compact. Their natural tendency is to spread.

Left: The center tree illustrates the natural way in which an Irish yew grows. The top of this tree has been cut. Notice that it fans out near the top.

Below: A trained Irish yew beside a garage door. The shape is already established.

is how yews are tied to make them assume a column e. Tie lengths of string around them like a succes- of belts, making sure that no branches escape the gs.

More yews tied to make column shapes; the tops of these have been cut.

Ivy trained into the shape of a life-size goat. Inside is a stiff wire armature. Care, pruning, and time did the rest. Created by Virginia Hughes, of Merryvale, San Francisco.

A life-size ivy dog standing in a planter box. He can be moved to any place in the garden. Created by Virginia Hughes, of Merryvale, San Francisco.

A bird shaped in ivy grows from a ceramic container. The ivy conceals a steel frame. The lower part is formed by ivy growing from the ceramic container. The bird is covered by potted ivy placed inside its frame.

This shape has been made with the same style and technique as the bird at the left, but the upper part is a plain sphere.

An ivy-covered light pole at an entry. This gardener wants an entry light, but he is also having some fun.

Here ivy has been trained and pruned to frame the entry of an old house in San Francisco. The ivy completely conceals its supports.

Tieing vines to make topiary

You can use vines such as ivy on a fence, as a ground cover, in containers, against a wall—in almost any way you can imagine.

There are many kinds of ivy, and they are easy to grow. When you select, look for one that most nearly fits your purpose. For instance, if you want to cover a large area, choose a large-leafed vine. For a small area or for a container, small leaves may be more appropriate.

English ivy is a very good choice for topiary. For one thing, it is hardy throughout the United States. For another, it is available in almost endless forms—small and large leaves, variegated foliage, slow- and fast-growing, open and dense foliage.

If you plan to make topiary in a container, you will need a framework. Frameworks are usually made of wire. You must then tie your vine so that it will follow the frame. Of course, the idea is to show as little as possible of your wire or string. Use as many plants as you think you need, and select short stems and leaves.

When you have achieved the desired form, you can then prune the vine so as to encourage a complete leafy covering.

Shaped plants in containers

Container plants have the advantage of being movable. You can place them where you like in the garden. A marguerite with the lower part cleaned out planted in a handsome container makes a distinctive display. The natural shape of marguerite is round, but any plant that becomes woody at its base can be trained into a standard.

Geraniums, too, can be shaped into standards. Here a stick supports the stem.

Low-growing flowering plants such as azaleas can also be trained as standards.

One might think that, having large leaves, the hydrangea is not really suitable material for a standard. But why not try it?

The wax leaf privet in this container is fully grown. Notice that a supporting stick is no longer necessary. Hampton Court, London.

Two junipers are being trained to grow together in a loop above a single container. They are tied to an oval wire frame. This will be interesting when the foliage has grown thicker.

A peacock-shaped eugenia grows in a clay pot. You can start like this, then improve the shape as time goes on.

Boxwood in a container has been trained in a swirled, spiral shape. It delights passers-by on a street in Copenhagen.

Trees in boxwood bases

Well-groomed street plants are the hallmark of a good residential area. Here is a good-looking arrangement. A dome-shaped waxed leaf tree stands handsomely on the sidewalk. Down below, square boxwoods neatly frame the planting and mark it off from the concrete sidewalk.

Top: A cone-shaped eugenia with a neatly pruned collar of boxwoods around the trunk.

Right: This idea is similar to the one pictured on the previous page. A young, unshaped tree is enclosed in a low-cut boxwood hedge. The base makes this rather ordinary tree look quite important.

A young eugenia beginning to form the shape the owner wants.

This eugenia has already developed into the desired shape. Not long ago it looked like the plant pictured on the left.

Local plants give the best results: Eugenia in San Francisco

When selecting plants to be shaped you have a wide choice. But if you choose plants you know do well in your area, it will be much easier to achieve the desired shape. No matter where you live in America, local nurserymen can supply plants suitable to the local climate that will give a good performance.

This mature eugenia has been shaped into a three-layer form. The top layer is a half-globe. If you would prefer a column, give it the same outline but do not cut it into layers.

In the San Francisco area eugenia is a species that grows fast and forms new foliage easily and quickly when trimmed so that you can achieve almost any shape you desire.

One of the advantages of eugenia (and mirror plant and pyracantha) is that it produces foliage so quickly that you can proceed by trial and error. If you do not like the first results, wait for new growth and then try again.

Many shapes from one species: Eugenia

This eugenia grows in a space between a property line and a path. Its shape is rectangular. Its purpose is to screen off an unattractive space at the side of the house. A visitor coming up the steps sees only the handsome shrub.

A eugenia was selected in this case because it is easy to grow and train and because it is good-looking all the year round.

This eugenia has been shaped to present a rising series of leaf clusters. It stands by its handsome self at the end of a Japanese-style stepping-stone pathway. To make this form, select large, strong branches and retain a cluster of leaves at the end of each. Prune unwanted branches and leaves growing near the trunk.

Only its owner could explain how this eugenia standing beside his garage came to have the shape it does. What he did was top his tree, then shape it into two parts, the top one wide and the bottom one smaller and cylindrical.

Shapes: Rectangles at entries

This entrance area is framed with hedges and shrubs all pruned on straight geometric lines. The pair of tall cypresses and the hedges harmonize with each other and with the design of the house. The overall effect is formal and tailored.

If you would like a more informal effect, just change the plants. Use camellias, bamboos, hollies, or conifers, and prune them unevenly.

Shrubs in a rectangular shape cover the flat expanse of a stairway wall. What you see here is a planting of four shrubs: two eugenias, a euonymus, and another eugenia.

Why not try a somewhat different shape? This privet hedge is more or less rectangular, but the ends are higher than the rest and the whole planting is slightly curved. The lower part is pruned to show some trunk. The purpose of this hedge is to keep people away from the driveway.

Variations on the sphere

The sphere is a fundamental shape. Pruning and trimming plants into round shapes is not easy, but these shapes are popular. Use the perfect sphere as a guide, but modify it to fit your own ideas: flatten it, squeeze it, halve it—push it around a little.

This five-foot-tall euonymus, trimmed to an almost complete globe and surrounded by boxwoods, is a great attention-getter.

Above: Semisphere of laurel combines with a great boulder to make a most unusual and attractive composition. The circular form echoes the spherical form and holds everything together.

Right: Careful pruning gives this three-foot-high holly placed between sidewalk and street the look of a leafy green ball. The bed in which it is planted is also round, in harmony.

A round, dark-green yew in front of a square shrub with variegated foliage.

Round shrubs beside steps

Round shrubs are often seen in front of homes. They are especially popular accompanying flights of steps.

In back of the yew is a waist-high hedge of variegated shrubs. The round yew is there simply to provide an accent.

Round yews on each side of a path leading to steps give a suggestion of a gate.

Similarly shaped pairs of shrubs are not always planted on each side of a path. Here you see two boxwoods side by side softening and concealing the stiff lines of the entry stairs.

This Japanese-style holly has a natural effect. Clusters of foliage are left at the end of the branches with generous open spaces between the leaf clusters.

Here is a six-layer boxwood. Some people might call this Japanese-style or pompon, but it has perhaps a more designed effect than is usual in Japan.

Variations on Japanese-style plant shaping

Foliage pruned into layers can be airy or dense, single or multiple, formal or informal. Although these shapes all have a Japanese flavor to a greater or lesser degree, only the holly is really Japanese. The others were photographed in the United States.

The holly, photographed in Beppu, Japan, has been shaped by pruning only (not trimming).

The boxwood formerly had a somewhat conventional shape. Because it has

This cypress is columnar, but it has also been cut into layers with spaces between them to give it a Japanese air.

This old cypress has one horizontal block of foliage floating above its two weathered trunks.

only a small area in which to grow, the owner and his gardener decided to change it to Japanese pompon. The forms are now fully established, and only trimming is needed to maintain the shape. The foliage has been divided into six separate elements, similar in general appearance but each with its own shape.

The shaped cypress has a comparatively natural look, but notice how the artist-pruner has divided it into many separate layers.

The aged cypress at the right has a single mass of foliage supported by two main trunks. These two weathered-looking supports are tied together at the bottom to prevent them from splitting apart and destroying the shape.

Shaping Japanese pines

Each well-designed Japanese garden has individuality, but all well-designed Japanese gardens have certain things in common. For one thing, the Japanese always provide privacy, usually by means of fences. Their gardens are designed to be enjoyed from a room within the house.

The plants are brought into the garden by man and shaped by man. One of the most suitable trees for a Japanese garden is pine, which the Japanese are remarkably successful in shaping.

Above: A beautifully shaped pine, which was transplanted a few years ago, in the garden of the mayor of Takamatsu City in Shikoku. *Below:* A shaped pine growing beside a street in Kyoto. The pine and rock harmonize well. This pine will always be a miniature.

This pine tree (behind the fences, right of center) in a private garden in Tokyo has been transplanted to its present location, and a pole is supporting it temporarily to protect it from the wind. Transplanting large trees is not unusual in Japan, and we saw similar transplanting methods in Pistoia, Italy.

Notice the role of bamboo in shaping the pine. Slender bamboo sticks are tied to the branches to direct their growth. This guidance, together with careful pruning, will make the tree a work of art within a few years.

Japanese style: The pompon shape

The photograph above was taken three years after this garden was redesigned in the Japanese manner. The floor plan of the garden was changed completely, but a few fully grown plants were kept and pruned in line with the Japanese approach to plant shaping. This tree had been growing more or less naturally. I decided to change it to a pompon style, which is more appropriate to a Japanese garden.

To make pompons, retain the strong branches and trim them until you have clumps of foliage at the ends. Shaping is really quite simple if you have a well-grown plant—and also an idea—to work with.

Asymmetrical balance

This pyracantha was planted twelve years ago. Until three years ago it grew naturally against this wall. Then its owner had a bright idea. Why not prune and train it into an unusual shape? He achieved this unusual form, which continues to delight his friends and passers-by.

The design is balanced in an unusual way. There are three major layers of leaves separated by open layers. Notice the middle layer; the right side is slightly heavier than the left. This compensates for the relative lack of weight on the right side in the layers above and below it. Each layer is unbalanced, but the whole composition is well balanced. Wouldn't you like to create a shape like this?

Foliage above dancing trunks

Occasionally you can emphasize a tree's trunk. The trunk or trunks can be straight, curved, in a group, even intertwined. No matter how intricate the line of trunks, if the foliage above them is balanced and harmonized, the general appearance can be most attractive.

Here a half-sphere of foliage is held by trunks with varied curves. Because this waxed leaf privet grows in an entrance area, it is especially well groomed.

The owner arranged the tree in this design after it was fully grown.

These two pictures of the same cotoneasters illustrate an example of shaped plants pruned to present a different appearance from different angles.

Foliage makes up one third of the structure. Notice how the dancing trunks contrast with the quiet top.

The picture on the right views the cotoneasters from the side. Here the shape looks as if it were cut completely in two. The cotoneasters have been shaped so that they grow parallel with the wall with some space in between.

Three layers against a wall

These two pictures illustrate an original plant composition that is worth your study. Notice how you see different shapes from the different angles.

This aged cedar, if left alone, would grow very tall. But it has been kept at a height of four feet to fit the garden scale.

Two-layer holly for accent

With patience, a careful eye, and your sharp pruning shears, you can make almost any compact shape you like and combine several shapes. A good shape pleases the eye and fits the space provided for it.

The variegated holly to the left is shaped as a two-layer compact standard. The large layer at the bottom and small one at the top float comfortably over the single slender trunk.

How many shaped trees and shrubs can you count in the photograph below? Each is handsomely done, but the chief success lies in the composition of the group.

An eccentric

You can often find interesting plants in books and magazines that give you ideas for shaping your own plants, but have you ever seen a plant quite like this one? We have seen many plants on our travels, and we consider this pyracantha a genuine original. We found it in San Francisco.

How did it come to have this shape? The plant itself suggested the idea. First the pyracantha was planted in front of a wall simply as an ornamental. It grew large and had to be pruned. Instead of just using shears in a routine manner, the owner noticed that the branches looked like fingers, and taking advantage of the growth habit of the plant, pruned it to reveal them.

Free form

Pruning can result in surprises. You start with a certain idea, and many times it will result in something quite different.

Today these pyracanthas bear little resemblance to their early appearance. Look at them. They do not look like any of the usual tree shapes but like an abstract foliage placement on the wall. There are two pyracanthas here, and their branches join at two places above the ground. They are growing up the wall; they surround one window; you wonder how they will look next year.

Let's close our book on this open-ended note. In shaping plants, just about anything can happen. It is up to you. Good luck and good pruning!